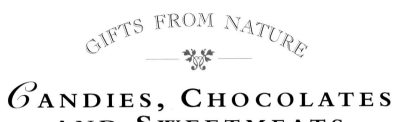

GIFTS FROM NATURE

Candies, Chocolates and Sweetmeats

GIFTS FROM NATURE

CANDIES, CHOCOLATES AND SWEETMEATS

Tempting treats to make for family and friends

SARAH AINLEY

LORENZ BOOKS

First published in 1998 by Lorenz Books

Lorenz Books is an imprint of
Anness Publishing Limited
Hermes House
88–89 Blackfriars Road
London SE1 8HA

This edition distributed in Canada by Raincoast Books, 8680 Cambie Street, Vancouver, British Columbia V6P 6M9

ISBN 1 85967 744 4

A CIP catalogue record for this book is available from the British Library

Publisher: Joanna Lorenz
Copy Editor: Christine Ingram
Designer: Lilian Lindblom
Illustrations: Anna Koska

Printed and bound in Singapore

1 3 5 7 9 10 8 6 4 2

ACKNOWLEDGEMENTS
Thanks to the following project contributors:
Jacqueline Clark, pp52–3; Stephanie Donaldson, pp12, 46, 47, 50; Tessa Evelegh, pp38–9, 61; Joanna Farrow, pp20–1, 42–3;
Christine France, pp11, 18, 24, 25, 29, 40; Judy Jackson, pp54, 62; Gilly Love, pp32, 33, 51; Sue Maggs, pp36; Norma Miller, pp28, 30–1, 41;
Janice Murfitt, pp10, 14–15, 26–7, 58–9; Pamela Westland, pp16, 19, 46, 56; Elizabeth Wolf-Cohen, pp17, 34–5, 37
Photographs by: Karl Adamson, Edward Allwright, Steve Baxter, Michelle Garrett, Nelson Hargreaves, David Jordan, Polly Wreford

C ONTENTS

INTRODUCTION

*W*hat could be more special than a gift of tempting treats? Home-made candies, chocolates, sweets and sweetmeats make perfect presents, and even more so if adorned with a hand-written label or piped initials for the personal touch that can make such a difference.

Christmas is an ideal time to make candied treats. Rich fudge and nutty toffee cookies are delicious served with steaming mulled wine, or wrapped in cellophane (plastic wrap) and hung as decorations from the Christmas tree. Velvet-smooth chocolates, of course, are welcome at any time of the year. Hand-made chocolates can be made to personal preference, whether it's for hard centres, mints, liqueurs or fresh cream truffles. Although off-puttingly expensive to buy, hand-made chocolates are relatively inexpensive to make, and are not in the least bit difficult. Once you have mastered the basic techniques, you can adapt the recipes for your own variations.

Sweetmeats too are a wonderful indulgence and make delightful gifts as well as pleasing treats to have in the store cupboard. All sorts of delicious fruits like peaches, pears, apricots and citrus fruits can be prepared and bottled with spices and spirits for a taste of summer at the end of the year. Discover how to make your own sugared decorations: marzipan fruits and sugared flowers are completely edible and add an attractive and original touch to cakes and desserts.

CANDIES

There is something delightfully nostalgic about home-made candies. Marshmallows, fudge and coconut ice were the favourites of our grandparents and are enjoyed just as much today. Home-made candies are wonderfully satisfying to make. Children will be only too enthusiastic to help in any way they can, and will be intrigued that such delectable

treats can be made from ordinary day-to-day ingredients. Like jams, candies are based on sugar syrups and keep extremely well – providing no-one is tempted to eat them straightaway!

FRUIT FONDANTS

❧

These chocolate-covered fondants are simple to make, yet look very professional. Fruit fondant is available from sugarcraft or specialist cake-making shops and comes in a variety of flavours, such as cherry, strawberry, orange and lime.

- 225 g (8 oz) plain (semisweet), milk or white chocolate, broken into squares
- 115 g (4 oz/1 cup)
- real fruit liquid fondant
- 15 ml (1 tbsp) melted plain, milk or white chocolate

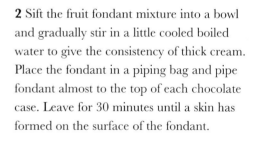

1 Polish the insides of 24 chocolate moulds with cotton wool. Place the chocolate in a bowl and set over a pan of barely simmering water. Heat gently until the chocolate has melted, and then spoon into each mould, reserving a little for sealing the creams. Use a small brush to sweep the chocolate up the sides of the moulds, then invert on to a sheet of greaseproof (wax) paper and leave to set.

2 Sift the fruit fondant mixture into a bowl and gradually stir in a little cooled boiled water to give the consistency of thick cream. Place the fondant in a piping bag and pipe fondant almost to the top of each chocolate case. Leave for 30 minutes until a skin has formed on the surface of the fondant.

3 Warm the remaining chocolate if necessary and spoon over the fondant so that it is level with the top. Chill until the chocolate is completely set and then invert the tray and press out the chocolates one by one. Place melted chocolate of a contrasting colour in a clean piping bag and pipe lines across the top of each chocolate. Allow to set completely before packing in a gift box, or arranging in an attractive serving bowl.

COGNAC AND GINGER CREAMS

These handsome chocolate candies make a wonderful gift. The mysterious dark exterior hides a glorious ginger and cognac cream filling.

- 300 g (11 oz) plain (semisweet) chocolate, broken into squares
- 45 ml (3 tbsp) double (heavy) cream
- 30 ml (2 tbsp) cognac
- 15 ml (1 tbsp) stem (preserved) ginger syrup
- 4 pieces stem (preserved) ginger, finely chopped
- crystallized (candied) ginger, to decorate

1 Polish the insides of 20 chocolate moulds with cotton wool. Place about two-thirds of the chocolate in a heatproof bowl, set over a pan of barely simmering water and heat until the chocolate has melted. Reserve a little of the remaining chocolate for sealing the creams.

2 Spoon a little chocolate into each mould. Using a small brush, sweep the chocolate up the sides of the moulds to coat evenly. Invert the moulds on to a sheet of greaseproof (wax) paper and leave until the chocolate has set.

3 Melt the remaining third of chocolate in a bowl and stir in the cream, cognac, ginger syrup and stem (preserved) ginger. Spoon into the chocolate-lined moulds. Warm the reserved chocolate until melted and spoon into each of the moulds to seal. Leave the chocolates in a cool place (not the fridge) until completely set.

4 To remove the chocolates, gently press them out on to a cool surface. Decorate with small pieces of crystallized (candied) ginger.

COCONUT ICE

Coconut ice is one of those old-fashioned sweets that is just as popular today as it was in our grandparents' childhood.
Make it for a delicious and original gift, parcelled up with cellophane (plastic wrap) into little squares.

- 1 coconut
- 450 g (1 lb/2 cups) granulated sugar
- 25 g (1 oz/2 tbsp) butter
- red food colouring

1 Break open the coconut, reserving the milk, and grate the coconut flesh. Place the sugar, about 120 ml (4 fl oz/½ cup) coconut milk and the butter in a saucepan and heat gently until the mixture begins to boil.

2 Slowly stir the grated coconut into the mixture in the saucepan and continue boiling for 10 minutes more. It is important to keep stirring the mixture as it boils.

3 Divide the mixture between two bowls and colour one pink using a little red food colouring. Press the uncoloured mixture into a greased 20 cm (8 in) square tin, smoothing the top evenly. Cover with a layer of pink coconut, smooth the top and leave until set.

4 Use a heavy knife to cut the coconut ice into 16 squares. Arrange on a plate to serve, or wrap each square individually in cellophane (plastic wrap) and tie with raffia.

MARSHMALLOWS

These marvellous mouthfuls of mousse are delicately flavoured with rose water to complement their pale pink colouring.
For orange mallows, flavour with orange flower water and colour with orange food colouring.

- 45 g (3 tbsp) icing (confectioners') sugar
- 45 g (3 tbsp) cornflour (cornstarch)
- 45 ml (3 tbsp) rose water
- 25 g (1 oz) powdered gelatine
- pink food colouring
- 450 g (1 lb/2 cups) granulated sugar
- 30 ml (2 tbsp) liquid glucose
- 2 egg whites

1 Lightly oil a 28 x 18 cm (11 x 7 in) Swiss roll tin (jelly roll pan). Sift together the icing (confectioners') sugar and cornflour (cornstarch) and use a little of this mixture to coat the bottom and sides of the tin. Tap the tin to coat evenly and shake out the excess.

2 Blend the rose water, gelatine and a drop of food colouring with 50 ml (3½ tbsp) cold water in a small heatproof bowl. Place the bowl over a saucepan of hot water and stir occasionally until the gelatine has dissolved.

3 Place the sugar, liquid glucose and 250 ml (8 fl oz/1 cup) boiling water in a heavy-based saucepan. Stir the mixture over a low heat to dissolve the sugar completely.

4 Bring the syrup to the boil and boil steadily, without stirring, until the temperature reaches 125°C (256°F) on a sugar thermometer. Remove the saucepan from the heat and stir in the gelatine mixture.

5 While the syrup is boiling, whisk the egg whites in a large bowl until stiff. Still whisking continuously, pour the syrup over the egg whites, and then continue whisking for about 3 minutes until the mixture is thick and foamy. At this stage add more food colouring if the mixture looks too pale.

6 Pour the mixture into the tin and allow to set for 4 hours. Sift some of the remaining icing sugar mixture over the marshmallow and spread the rest over a baking (cookie) sheet. Ease the mixture away from the tin and invert on to a board. Cut into squares, coating the sides with the icing sugar mixture. Pack the marshmallows in a pretty box.

CRANBERRY FUDGE

This rich candy comes from Scotland where it is called "Butter tablet". You can make a variety of flavours by using chopped pecans, crystallized (candied) ginger or other candied fruits instead of cranberries.

- 115 g (4 oz/¼ cup) fresh cranberries
- 900 g (2 lb/4 cups) granulated sugar
- 50 g (2 oz/4 tbsp) unsalted (sweet) butter
- 175 ml (6 fl oz/¾ cup) milk
- 15 ml (1 tbsp) golden (corn) syrup
- 200 g (7 oz) can condensed milk

1 Wash the cranberries, discarding any that are bruised or discoloured. Pat dry and set aside. Grease a 28 x 18 cm (11 x 7in) Swiss roll tin (jelly roll pan).

2 Place the sugar, butter, milk and golden (corn) syrup in a heavy-based saucepan and bring slowly to the boil, stirring constantly. Add the condensed milk, return to the boil and boil for 20 minutes further, stirring continuously, until the mixture reaches 125°C (256°F) on a sugar thermometer, or until a spoonful of the mixture, dropped into a cup of cold water, sets hard.

3 Remove the saucepan from the heat and stir in the cranberries. Pour the mixture into the prepared tin and leave to set. Mark the fudge into squares just before it hardens. When the fudge is completely cold, cut it into squares, using a heavy kitchen knife, and store in an airtight container. Serve as a tea-time treat or pack in a pretty box for a gift.

NUTTY FUDGE RIBBON

This luscious fudge can be stored in an airtight container in the fridge for up to two weeks – although it probably won't last that long!

- 600 g (1 lb 6 oz) fine quality white chocolate, broken into squares
- 400 g (14 oz) can condensed milk
- 15 ml (1 tbsp) vanilla essence (extract)
- 7.5 ml (1½ tsp) lemon juice
- 225 g (8 oz/2 cups) hazelnuts or pecans, chopped (optional)
- 225 g (8 oz) plain (semisweet) chocolate
- 40 g (1½ oz/3 tbsp) unsalted (sweet) butter, cubed
- salt

1 Line a 20 cm (8 in) square baking tin (pan) with foil and brush the bottom and sides with a little oil. Place the white chocolate and condensed milk in a saucepan and heat very gently until the chocolate has melted, stirring all the time. Remove from the heat and stir in the vanilla essence (extract), lemon juice, a pinch of salt and the nuts, if using. Pour half the mixture into the prepared tin and smooth the top. Chill in the fridge for 15 minutes.

2 Meanwhile, break 175 g (6 oz) of the plain (semisweet) chocolate and the butter into a heatproof bowl set over a pan of barely simmering water and heat gently until the chocolate and butter have melted, stirring occasionally. Cool slightly, then pour over the white layer of fudge. Chill for 15 minutes.

3 Gently warm the remaining white chocolate mixture in a saucepan until melted, then pour over the set chocolate layer, smoothing the top with a palette knife. Chill for 2–4 hours, until the white chocolate has set completely.

4 Transfer the fudge to a cutting board and remove the foil. Cut the fudge into 24 squares and then cut each square into triangles. Melt the remaining plain chocolate in a saucepan and pipe over each triangle. Leave to set.

Almond Triangles

This sinfully rich concoction makes an irresistible after-dinner indulgence.

- 115 g (4 oz) plain (semisweet) chocolate
- 50 g (2 oz/4 tbsp) unsalted (sweet) butter
- 1 egg white
- 115 g (4 oz/½ cup) caster (superfine) sugar
- 50 g (2 oz/½ cup) ground almonds
- 75 g (3 oz/¾ cup) chopped toasted almonds
- 5 tbsp (⅓ cup) chopped lemon candied peel

For the coating:
- 175 g (6 oz) white chocolate, broken into squares
- 25 g (1 oz/2 tbsp) unsalted (sweet) butter
- 115 g (4 oz/1 cup) flaked (slivered) almonds, toasted

1 Break the plain (semisweet) chocolate into squares and place in a heatproof bowl, set over a saucepan of barely simmering water. Add the unsalted (sweet) butter to the pan. Heat gently until the chocolate and butter have completely melted, stirring occasionally.

2 Whisk the egg white with the sugar until stiff. Gradually beat in the melted chocolate, then stir in the ground almonds, chopped toasted almonds and candied peel. Transfer the mixture to a large sheet of non-stick baking paper (parchment) and shape into a thick roll.

3 As the mixture cools, use the paper to press the roll firmly into a triangular shape. Twist the paper over the triangular roll and chill in the fridge until completely set.

4 Meanwhile, make the coating: melt the white chocolate with the butter in a heatproof bowl over a pan of hot water. Unwrap the chocolate roll and spread the white chocolate quickly over the surface. Press the almonds in a thin even coating over the chocolate, working quickly before the chocolate sets. Chill again until firm, then cut into thin slices before packing in a decorative box.

HONEY AND NUT CLUSTER

This popular Italian candy is known as "Torrone". For an unusual touch at Christmas, wrap it in sparkly paper or a pretty cotton fabric and fix to the Christmas tree as a special decoration.

- 115 g (4 oz/¾ cup) blanched almonds
- 115 g (4 oz/1 cup) shelled hazelnuts

- 2 egg whites
- 115 g (4 oz/⅓ cup) clear honey
- 115 g (4 oz/½ cup) caster (superfine) sugar

1 Preheat the oven to 110°C (225°F/Gas 1/4). Meanwhile, measure and cut a sheet of non-stick baking paper (parchment) to line a 20 cm (8 in) square cake tin (pan). Set the tin aside.

2 Spread the nuts in a layer on a baking (cookie) sheet and toast them in the oven for 30 minutes until golden. Allow the nuts to cool slightly, then chop them roughly, using a heavy knife. Whisk the egg whites until stiff and stir in the chopped nuts.

3 Put the honey and sugar in a heavy-based saucepan and bring to the boil. Stir in the nut mixture and continue cooking over a moderate heat for about 10 minutes. Turn the mixture into the prepared tin, using a palette knife to smooth the surface.

4 Cover with another piece of non-stick baking paper, held in place with weights (such as food cans). Chill in the fridge for 2 days. Cut the Torrone into 1.25 x 5 cm (½ x 2 in) squares. Wrap in non-stick baking paper and keep in the fridge until ready to serve.

CANDY NECKLACES

These novelty necklaces are made from tiny gingerbread cookies, decorated and threaded onto lengths of ribbon. Arrange in a pretty, tissue-lined box for presentation.

For the gingerbread:
- 115 g (4 oz/½ cup) unsalted (sweet) butter, softened
- 50 g (2 oz/¼ cup) caster (superfine) sugar
- 1 egg
- 125 g (4¼ oz/½ cup) black treacle (molasses)
- 225 g (8 oz/2 cups) plain (all-purpose) flour

- 5 ml (1 tsp) ground ginger
- 2.5 ml (½ tsp) ground cloves

For the decoration:
- 225 g (8 oz/ 2 cups) icing (confectioners') sugar
- pink food colouring
- selection of small sweets (candies)
- pink, blue or white ribbon

*U*se licorice whips instead of lengths of ribbon for threading the cookies, to make the necklaces totally edible — perfect for presenting as party favours.

1 For the gingerbread, cream together the butter and sugar until pale and fluffy. Beat in the egg and black treacle (molasses). Sift the flour, ginger and cloves and then beat into the egg and black treacle to make a stiff paste. Turn out on to a floured surface and knead lightly until smooth. Wrap in cellophane (plastic wrap) and chill for about 30 minutes.

2 Preheat the oven to 180°C (350°F/Gas 4). Grease two baking (cookie) sheets. Roll out slightly more than half the gingerbread mixture on a lightly floured surface to a thickness of 1 cm (½ in). Cut out star shapes, using a cutter, then transfer the shapes to a baking sheet. Make a large hole in the centre of each shape with a metal skewer.

3 Mix the trimmings with the remaining dough and roll into a thick sausage, about 2 cm (¾ in) in diameter. Cut into 1 cm (½ in) slices, place on the second baking sheet and make a hole in the centre. Place the baking sheets in the oven and bake for 8 minutes. Remake the holes while still warm, then transfer the cookies to a wire rack to cool.

4 Blend the icing (confectioners') sugar with warm water to make a paste, then place half the quantity in a piping bag and pipe around the edges of the stars. Colour the remaining icing pale pink and put in a piping bag fitted with a star nozzle. Pipe stars on to the round cookies and decorate with sweets (candies). Let dry, then thread the cookies on to ribbon.

CHOCOLATES

As any chocolate lover will know, hand-made chocolates are quite simply the best chocolates of all. Made with favourite fillings of nuts, fresh cream, liqueurs or ginger, they are a devilish treat and the *pièce de résistance* at the end of a dinner party. The chocolates included here are surprisingly simple to make but the end results look impressive, and make

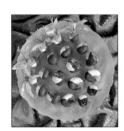

wonderful gifts if you can bear to give them away. Always try to use a fine quality plain (semisweet) chocolate, adding variation with milk and white chocolate.

CHOCOLATE FONDANT HEARTS

If you're looking for a gift for your Valentine, look no further. For a really romantic touch, pipe both your initials entwined on top of each chocolate.

- 60 ml (4 tbsp) liquid glucose
- 50 g (2 oz) plain (semisweet) chocolate, plus extra for decorating
- 50 g (2 oz) white chocolate, plus extra for decorating
- 1 egg white
- 450 g (1 lb/3 cups) icing (confectioners') sugar, sifted, plus extra for dusting

1 Divide the glucose between two heatproof bowls. Place each bowl over a pan of barely simmering water and heat gently. Break the two types of chocolate into pieces. Add the plain (semisweet) chocolate to one bowl and the white chocolate to the other and continue to heat until melted.

2 Remove both bowls of chocolate from the heat and set them aside to cool. Whisk the egg white until stiff, then add one-third to each bowl, reserving the remaining third. Divide the icing (confectioners') sugar equally between the bowls and stir in thoroughly to mix.

3 Turn the mixture out of the bowl and knead separately, with your hands, until smooth and pliable. Dust a work surface with icing sugar and roll out each piece to a 3 mm (⅛ in) thickness.

4 Brush the surface of the dark chocolate fondant with the remaining egg white and place the white chocolate fondant on top. Roll the surface with a rolling pin to press the pieces together.

5 Using a heart-shaped cutter, stamp out about 50 hearts from the fondant. Melt the extra plain and white chocolate and pipe or drizzle over the top of each chocolate heart. Leave to set before packing in a box.

PEPPERMINT CHOCOLATE STICKS

Cover mint chocolate boxes with coloured foil and pack with these delicate peppermint sticks for an elegant gift.
If you prefer to keep them for yourself, they'll make the perfect partner for after-dinner coffee.

- 115 g (4 oz/½ cup) granulated sugar
- 2.5 ml (½ tsp) peppermint essence (extract)
- 200 g (7 oz) plain
- (semisweet) chocolate
- 60 ml (4 tbsp) desiccated (shredded) coconut, toasted

1 Lightly oil a large baking (cookie) sheet. Place the sugar and 150 ml (¼ pint/⅔ cup) water in a heavy-based saucepan and heat gently, stirring occasionally, until the sugar has dissolved completely.

2 Bring to the boil and boil rapidly without stirring until the syrup reaches 138°C (280°F) on a sugar thermometer. Remove the pan from the heat, add the peppermint essence (extract), then pour on to the greased baking sheet and leave until set and completely cold.

3 Break the peppermint mixture into a bowl, using a rolling pin to crush it into small pieces.

4 Break the chocolate into a heatproof bowl and set over a pan of barely simmering water. Heat gently until the chocolate has melted and then remove from the heat and stir in the mint pieces and desiccated (shredded) coconut.

5 Lay a 30 x 25 cm (12 x 10 in) sheet of non-stick baking paper (parchment) on a flat surface. Spread the chocolate mixture over the paper, leaving a narrow border all the way around, to make a rectangle measuring about 25 x 20 cm (10 x 8 in). Leave to set. When the chocolate is firm, use a sharp knife to cut into thin sticks about 6 cm (2½ in) long.

CHOCOLATE BOXES

These tiny chocolate boxes make the ideal containers for hand-made chocolates or sweets. Use white or milk chocolate with dark trimmings to vary the theme.

- 225 g (8 oz) plain (semisweet) or milk chocolate
- 50 g (2 oz) white chocolate
- hand-made chocolates or sweets (candies)

1 Line a large baking (cookie) sheet with non-stick baking paper (parchment). Break the plain (semisweet) or milk chocolate into a heatproof bowl and set over a pan of barely simmering water. Heat the chocolate gently until melted, then remove from the heat.

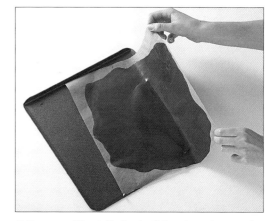

2 Reserve 15 ml (1 tbsp) of the chocolate and set aside. Pour the remaining chocolate over the baking paper and quickly spread it to the edges, using a palette knife. Pick up two corners of the baking paper and drop: do this several times on each side, to level the surface.

3 Leave the chocolate until almost set but still pliable. Place a clean piece of non-stick baking paper on the surface, invert the chocolate sheet and peel away the baking paper. Use a ruler and scalpel or sharp knife to measure and cut the chocolate sheet into 16 squares of 5 cm (2 in) to form the sides of the boxes. Measure and cut out 8 squares of 5.5 cm (2¼ in) for the lids and bases of each of the boxes.

4 To assemble the boxes, warm the reserved chocolate and paint a little along the edges of one of the chocolate squares, using a fine brush. Place the side pieces of the box in position one at a time, brushing over the edges with the melted chocolate to join the four squares together to form a box. Leave the assembled box to set. Meanwhile, repeat with the remaining three boxes.

5 Melt the white chocolate and spoon it into a greaseproof (wax) paper piping bag. Pipe 20 chocolate loops on to a sheet of baking paper and leave them to set.

6 Fill the boxes with handmade chocolates or sweets (candies) and top with the remaining chocolate square. Decorate the sides of the boxes with chocolate loops, each secured with a bead of white chocolate. Alternatively, wrap a ribbon carefully around each box and tie with a bow. Pack in a decorative gift box.

COINTREAU CHOCOLATE COLETTES

Small chocolate cases, filled with swirled chocolate and orange liqueur cream, make a sweet surprise for a friend or lover.

- 115 g (4 oz) plain (semisweet) chocolate
- icing (confectioners') sugar, for dusting

For the filling:
- 65 g (2½ oz) plain (semisweet) chocolate
- 25 g (1 oz/2 tbsp) unsalted (sweet) butter
- 30 ml (2 tbsp) Cointreau or orange liqueur
- 60 ml (4 tbsp) double (heavy) cream, whipped

1 Break the chocolate into a heatproof bowl and set over a pan of barely simmering water. Heat gently until the chocolate has melted.

2 Brush the insides of 14 *petit four* cases with a thin coating of melted chocolate and leave to set. Repeat three or four times. When finally set, carefully peel off the paper cases.

3 Make the filling. Melt the chocolate and butter together in a heatproof bowl over a saucepan of simmering water.

4 Remove the bowl from the heat. When cool, but still liquid, stir in the Cointreau or orange liqueur and fold in the whipped cream.

5 Chill the mixture until firm, then pipe it into the chocolate cases. Leave to set before dusting lightly with icing (confectioners') sugar.

RICH CHOCOLATE PISTACHIO FUDGE

This heavenly chocolate fudge will become an instant success with family and friends.

- 250 g (9 oz/ generous 1 cup) granulated sugar
- 400 g (14 oz) can condensed milk
- 50 g (2 oz/4 tbsp) unsalted (sweet) butter
- 5ml (1 tsp) vanilla essence (extract)
- 115 g (4 oz) plain (semisweet) chocolate, grated
- 75 g (3 oz/¾ cup) pistachios, almonds or hazelnuts

1 Grease an 18 cm (7 in) square cake tin (pan) and line with non-stick baking paper (parchment). Mix the sugar, condensed milk and butter in a heavy-based saucepan and heat gently, stirring occasionally until the sugar has dissolved completely.

2 Bring the mixture to the boil, stirring occasionally, and boil until it reaches 119°C (238°F) on a sugar thermometer. Remove the pan from the heat and beat in the vanilla essence (extract), grated chocolate and nuts. Beat until the mixture is smooth and creamy.

3 Pour the mixture into the prepared cake tin and spread evenly. Leave until just set, then mark into squares. Leave to set completely before cutting the squares and removing them from the tin. Store the fudge in an airtight container in a cool place or wrap loosely in greaseproof (wax) paper and pack in a gift box.

BOURBON BALLS

This American delicacy laces biscuit and pecan truffles with bourbon.

- 175 g (6 oz) Nice biscuits
- 115 g (4 oz/1 cup) pecan nuts, chopped
- 30 ml (2 tbsp) cocoa powder
- 75 g (3 oz/¼ cup) icing (confectioners') sugar, sifted
- 30 ml (2 tbsp) clear honey
- 120 ml (4 fl oz/½ cup) bourbon

1 Put the biscuits in a plastic bag and crush them finely, using a rolling pin. Tip the crumbs into a bowl and add the chopped nuts, cocoa powder and half of the icing (confectioners') sugar. Add the honey and bourbon. Stir until the mixture forms a stiff paste, adding more bourbon if necessary.

2 Shape the mixture into small balls. Place the balls on a plate and chill in the fridge until firm.

3 Roll the balls in the remaining icing sugar. Chill for 15 minutes and roll again in the sugar. Store in an airtight container or pack in a decorative gift box.

MOCHA TRUFFLES WITH CAFE NOIR

The combination of coffee liqueur and chocolate is irresistible. Give these as a gift and you'll be a friend for life.

- 175 g (6 oz) plain (semisweet) chocolate
- 50 g (2 oz/4 tbsp) unsalted (sweet) butter
- 10 ml (2 tsp) instant coffee granules
- 30 ml (2 tbsp) double (heavy) cream
- 225 g (8 oz/4 cups) Madeira cake crumbs
- 50 g (2 oz/½ cup) ground almonds
- 30 ml (2 tbsp) Café Noir liqueur
- cocoa powder, chocolate vermicelli (sprinkles) or ground almonds, to coat

1 Break the chocolate into a heatproof bowl with the butter and instant coffee. Set the bowl over a pan of barely simmering water and heat gently until the chocolate and butter have melted and the coffee has dissolved.

2 Remove from the heat and stir in the cream, cake crumbs, ground almonds and Café Noir.

3 Chill the mixture until firm. Shape into small balls, roll in cocoa powder, chocolate vermicelli (sprinkles) or ground almonds, and place in foil *petit four* cases. Pack the truffles in gift boxes or arrange them on a serving plate.

SWEDISH ROSE CHOCOLATES

This rich chocolate sweet is simple to make and completely delicious. It is a popular Swedish Christmas treat, where it might be offered as a gift or served on Christmas Eve.

- 150 g (5 oz) plain (semisweet) chocolate
- 30 ml (2 tbsp) ground almonds
- 30 ml (2 tbsp) caster (superfine) sugar
- 2 egg yolks
- 10 ml (2 tsp) strong brewed coffee
- 15 ml (1 tbsp) dark rum
- 15 ml (1 tbsp) rose water
- 40 g (1½ oz/ ¼ cup) chocolate vermicelli (sprinkles)
- crystallized rose petals, for decoration

1 Grate the chocolate finely or grind in batches in a coffee or spice mill. Place in a bowl and add the ground almonds, caster (superfine) sugar, egg yolks, coffee and rum.

2 Roll the mixture into balls by rolling small teaspoonfuls between your fingers. Chill well.

3 Dip each of the chocolate balls into the rose water, then roll in the chocolate vermicelli (sprinkles) until completely coated.

4 Wrap the chocolate balls individually in cellophane (plastic wrap) tied with natural raffia before packing them in decorative boxes, or pile them high on a serving plate, sprinkled with crystallized rose petals.

For crystallized rose petals, coat clean and dry petals with a thin and even layer of beaten egg white and, working quickly, sprinkle with sifted icing (confectioners') sugar. Allow the petals to dry for 30 minutes on a wire rack. The petals will keep for up to a week, stored in an airtight container between layers of paper towels.

ROSE PETAL TRUFFLES

These glamorous chocolates are fun to make as a Valentine gift or for an engagement.

- 500 g (1¼ lb) plain (semisweet) chocolate
- 300 ml (½ pint/ 1¼ cups) double (heavy) cream
- 15 ml (1 tbsp) rose water
- 2 drops rose essential oil
- 250 g (9 oz) plain (semisweet) chocolate, for coating
- crystallized rose petals, for decoration

1 Break the chocolate into a bowl or into the top of a double boiler. Add the cream and set over a pan of barely simmering water. Heat gently until the chocolate has melted, stirring.

2 Mix in the rose water and essential oil, then pour into a baking tin (pan) lined with non-stick baking paper (parchment) and let cool.

3 When almost firm, take teaspoonfuls of the chocolate and shape into balls, using your hands. Chill the truffles until they are hard.

4 Melt the chocolate for the coating over a pan of simmering water. Skewer a truffle and dip it into the melted chocolate. Decorate with a crystallized rose petal before the chocolate has set, then leave on a sheet of non-stick baking paper to dry completely. Scatter with crystallized rose petals before packing in a box.

CHOCOLATE BOX WITH CARAMEL MOUSSE AND BERRIES

The fabulous taste and impressive presentation make this a wonderful centrepiece for just about any special occasion dinner.

- 275 g (10 oz) plain (semisweet) chocolate

For the mousse:
- 4 x 50 g (2 oz) chocolate-coated caramel bars, coarsely chopped
- 20 ml (1½ tbsp) milk
- 350 ml (12 fl oz/ 1½ cups) double (heavy) cream
- 1 egg white

For the caramel shards:
- 90 g (3½ oz/½ cup) granulated sugar

For the topping:
- 115 g (4 oz) white chocolate
- 350 ml (12 fl oz/ 1½ cups) double (heavy) cream
- 450 g (1 lb) mixed berries, such as raspberries and blackberries

1 Prepare the chocolate box. Line a 23 cm (9 in) square baking tin (pan) with a single piece of foil, pressing firmly against the edges to make the foil as smooth as possible.

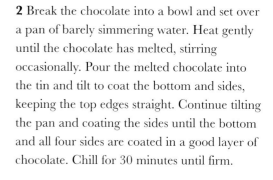

2 Break the chocolate into a bowl and set over a pan of barely simmering water. Heat gently until the chocolate has melted, stirring occasionally. Pour the melted chocolate into the tin and tilt to coat the bottom and sides, keeping the top edges straight. Continue tilting the pan and coating the sides until the bottom and all four sides are coated in a good layer of chocolate. Chill for 30 minutes until firm.

3 Put the caramel bars and milk in a heatproof bowl. Place over a pan of simmering water and heat until melted, stirring occasionally. Remove the bowl from the heat and cool for about 10 minutes, stirring once or twice. In a separate bowl, whip the cream until soft peaks form. Stir a spoonful of cream into the caramel mixture, then fold in the remaining cream. Whisk the egg white in a clean bowl until just stiff; fold into the mousse mixture and then pour the mixture into the box. Chill in the fridge for several hours.

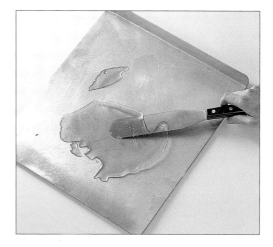

4 Meanwhile, prepare the caramel shards. Lightly oil a baking (cookie) sheet. Place the sugar in a pan with 65 ml (4½ tbsp) water. Heat gently to dissolve the sugar, then increase the heat and bring to the boil. Allow to boil for 5 minutes, without stirring, until the sugar turns a pale golden colour. Wearing oven gloves (caramel is dangerously hot), pour the caramel on to the oiled sheet, spreading it with a palette knife to form an even layer. Cool completely, then, using a metal palette knife, lift off the baking sheet and break into pieces.

5 To make the topping, break the white chocolate into a bowl and add 120 ml (4 fl oz/ ½ cup) of the cream. Set over a pan of simmering water and heat until the chocolate has melted, stirring. Allow to cool to room temperature, stirring occasionally. Whip the remaining cream until peaks form. Stir a spoonful of cream into the white chocolate mixture and then fold in the remainder. Remove the mousse-filled box from the tin and peel off the foil, first from the sides, then the bottom. Slide on to a serving plate.

6 Spoon the chocolate cream mixture into a piping bag and pipe a decoration over the top of the chocolate box. Arrange the berries over the surface and decorate with caramel shards.

CHOCOLATE KISSES

These little chocolate biscuits are a novel treat at Christmas, and will make a welcome change from traditional seasonal fare.

- 75 g (3 oz) plain (semisweet) chocolate
- 75 g (3 oz) white chocolate
- 115 g (4 oz/½ cup) unsalted (sweet) butter
- 115 g (4 oz/8 tbsp) caster (superfine) sugar
- 2 eggs
- 225 g (8 oz/2 cups) plain flour
- icing (confectioners') sugar, for decoration

1 Break the plain (semisweet) and white chocolate into separate heatproof bowls. Set over pans of barely simmering water and heat until the chocolate has melted, stirring occasionally. Let cool.

2 Whisk together the butter and caster (superfine) sugar until pale and fluffy. Beat in the eggs, one at a time, then sift in the flour and mix together well.

3 Halve the mixture and divide it between the two bowls of chocolate, mixing the chocolate in thoroughly. Turn out the mixture and knead each dough until smooth and pliable. Wrap in cellophane (plastic wrap) and chill for 1 hour in the fridge. Preheat the oven to 190°C (375°F/Gas 5).

4 Shape rounded teaspoonfuls of dough into balls, rolling them in the palms of your hands to make neat shapes. Arrange the balls on greased baking (cookie) sheets and bake in the oven for 10–12 minutes. Dust with sifted icing (confectioners') sugar and transfer to a wire rack to cool.

DOUBLE CHOCOLATE-DIPPED FRUIT

Just about any kind of fruit can be dipped in chocolate for a truly mouth-watering feast.

- 24 fruit pieces, such as strawberries, cherries, orange segments, large seedless grapes, stoned dates or cape gooseberries
- 115 g (4 oz) white chocolate
- 115 g (4 oz) plain (semisweet) chocolate

1 Clean and prepare the fruit. Rinse under running water, dry well and set on kitchen paper to absorb any remaining moisture.

2 Break the white chocolate into a bowl and set over a pan of barely simmering water. Heat gently until melted, then remove from the heat and cool to tepid, stirring frequently. Line a baking (cookie) sheet with non-stick baking paper (parchment). Holding the fruit by the stem or from one end and at an angle, dip about two-thirds of the fruit into the chocolate. Allow any excess chocolate to drip off and place on the prepared baking sheet. Leave the fruit in the fridge until the chocolate has set completely.

3 Break the plain (semisweet) chocolate into a heatproof bowl and set over a pan of barely simmering water. Heat gently until the chocolate has melted, stirring occasionally. Remove from the heat and cool to tepid.

4 Take each white chocolate-coated fruit and, holding by the stem or from one end and at the opposite angle, dip the bottom third into the chocolate, creating a chevron effect. Set the fruit on the baking sheet and chill for at least 15 minutes until set. Remove from the fridge 10–15 minutes before serving. Dipped fruit is best eaten on the day it is made.

GINGERED TRUFFLES

Wonderfully creamy, these rich chocolate truffles are flecked with ginger, coated in dark chocolate and piped with melted white chocolate: a truly impressive gift.

- 150 ml (¼ pint/ ⅔ cup) double (heavy) cream
- 400 g (14 oz) plain (semisweet) chocolate, broken into squares
- 25 g (1 oz) butter
- 25 g (1 oz/2 tbsp)

- brandy
- 30 ml (2 tbsp) glacé (candied) ginger, finely chopped
- 15 ml (1 tbsp) cocoa powder
- 50 g (2 oz) white chocolate, broken into squares

1 Place the cream in a heavy-based saucepan and bring to the boil. Remove from the heat and add 150 g (5 oz) of the plain (semisweet) chocolate and the butter. Leave to stand for 5 minutes, stirring, until the chocolate and butter have melted. Return the pan to the heat for a few seconds if the chocolate and butter don't melt completely. Stir in the brandy, then, using an electric whisk, beat for 4–5 minutes, until the mixture is thick. Add 15 ml (1 tbsp) of the glacé (candied) ginger and stir well. Cover and chill for 2–3 hours until firm.

2 For the decoration, dip a teaspoon of the mixture in the cocoa powder and roll it into a ball, using your hands. Set aside and continue until all the mixture is used up. Freeze the truffles for 30 minutes until hard.

3 Place the remaining dark chocolate in a bowl set over a saucepan of simmering water. Heat until melted, stirring occasionally. Holding a truffle on a fork, spoon the melted chocolate over it until completely coated.

4 Carefully transfer to a baking (cookie) sheet lined with non-stick baking paper (parchment). Sprinkle the remaining glacé ginger over the truffles and leave to cool and harden. Melt the white chocolate and spoon into a greaseproof (wax) paper piping bag. Pipe squiggly lines over the truffles and leave in the fridge to harden. Pack the truffles into *petit four* cases and arrange in boxes. Cover with a lid or cellophane (plastic wrap) and tie with a decorative ribbon.

CHOCOLATE NUT BRITTLE

This is a sensational chocolate candy – a favourite with children and adults alike.

- butter, for greasing
- 115 g (4 oz/1 cup) pecan nuts and whole almonds
- 115 g (4 oz/½ cup)

- caster (superfine) sugar
- 200 g (7 oz) plain (semisweet) chocolate

1 Lightly grease a baking (cookie) sheet with butter. Mix the nuts, sugar and 60 ml (4 tbsp) water in a heavy-based saucepan. Place over a low heat and heat gently, without boiling, until the sugar has dissolved, stirring frequently.

2 Bring the mixture to the boil, then lower the heat and boil, without stirring, until the mixture reaches 151°C (304°F) on a sugar thermometer, or turns a rich golden brown.

3 Remove the saucepan from the heat and carefully tip the mixture on to the prepared baking sheet, spreading it evenly with a palette knife. Leave until completely cold and hard.

4 Break the brittle into bite-size pieces. Melt the chocolate in a heatproof bowl over a pan of barely simmering water, stirring until smooth. Dip the pieces of brittle into the melted chocolate and then set aside on a sheet of non-stick baking paper (parchment) to set.

These look best in rough chunks, so don't worry if the pieces break unevenly or if there are gaps in the chocolate coating.

MINI FLORENTINES WITH GRAND MARNIER

Orange liqueur adds a touch of luxury to these ever-popular biscuits.

- 50 g (2 oz/⅓ cup) light brown sugar
- 15 ml (1 tbsp) clear honey
- 15 ml (1 tbsp) Grand Marnier
- 50 g (2 oz/4 tbsp) unsalted (sweet) butter
- 40 g (1½ oz/3 tbsp) plain (all-purpose) flour
- 25 g (1 oz/¼ cup) hazelnuts and almonds, chopped
- 50 g (2 oz/¼ cup) glacé (candied) cherries, chopped
- 115 g (4 oz) plain (semisweet) chocolate, broken into squares

1 Preheat the oven to 180°C (350°F/Gas 4) and line three or four baking (cookie) sheets with non-stick baking paper (parchment). Put the sugar, honey, Grand Marnier and unsalted (sweet) butter in a small saucepan and melt over a low heat, stirring occasionally.

2 Remove the saucepan from the heat and tip in the flour, chopped hazelnuts, almonds and glacé (candied) cherries. Stir the mixture well.

3 Spoon small heaps of the mixture on to the baking sheets and bake for 10 minutes until golden brown. Leave the biscuits on the baking sheets until the edges begin to harden a little, then transfer to a wire rack to cool.

4 Melt the chocolate in a bowl set over a pan of barely simmering water and spread a little over one side of each florentine. As the chocolate begins to set, drag a fork through to give wavy lines. Leave to set completely.

DECORATED CHOCOLATE LEBKUCHEN

Wrapped in paper or beautifully boxed, these decorated Lebkuchen cookies make a lovely present.
Don't make them too far in advance as the chocolate will gradually discolour.

For the Lebkuchen:
- 115 g (4 oz/½ cup) unsalted (sweet) butter, softened
- 50 g (2 oz/¼ cup) soft brown sugar
- 1 egg, beaten
- 350 g (12 oz/1 cup) black treacle (molasses)
- 350 g (12 oz/ 3 cups) self-raising flour
- 5 ml (1 tsp) ground ginger
- 2.5 ml (½ tsp) ground cloves
- pinch of chilli powder

For the decoration:
- 115 g (4 oz) plain (semisweet) chocolate
- 115 g (4 oz) milk chocolate
- 115 g (4 oz) white chocolate
- chocolate vermicelli (sprinkles)
- cocoa powder or icing (confectioners') sugar, for dusting

1 For the Lebkuchen, cream together the butter and sugar until pale and fluffy. Beat in the egg and black treacle (molasses). Sift the flour, ginger, cloves and chilli powder and then beat into the egg and treacle mixture to make a stiff paste. Turn out on to a lightly floured surface and knead lightly until smooth. Wrap the dough in cellophane (plastic wrap) and chill in the fridge for about 30 minutes.

2 Grease two baking (cookie) sheets. Roll out just over half the Lebkuchen mixture to 1 cm (½ in) thickness. Cut out heart shapes using a 4 cm (1½ in) heart-shaped cutter and arrange on the baking sheets. Gather the trimmings with the remaining dough and cut into 20 pieces. Roll into balls and place on the baking sheets. Flatten each one slightly and then chill the sheets for 30 minutes.

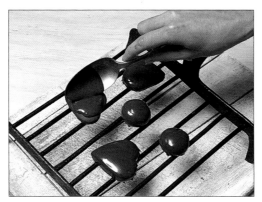

3 Preheat the oven to 180°C (350°F/Gas 4), then cook the biscuits for about 8–10 minutes until firm. Cool on a wire rack. Break the plain (semisweet) chocolate into pieces and melt it in a heatproof bowl set over a saucepan of barely simmering water. Melt the milk and white chocolate in separate bowls. When melted, spoon a little of each chocolate into three greaseproof (wax) paper piping bags.

4 Spoon a little of the plain chocolate over a third of the cookies, spreading it with the back of the spoon or a palette knife to cover them completely. Drizzle fine lines of white chocolate over a few of the plain chocolate-coated cookies and scatter the remainder with the chocolate vermicelli (sprinkles).

5 Coat the remaining cookies with the milk and white chocolate and decorate some of these with chocolate from the piping bags, contrasting the colours. Sprinkle the remaining chocolate-coated cookies with vermicelli, or dust them with the cocoa powder or icing (confectioners') sugar. Allow to set completely before packing in a gift box.

SWEETMEATS

Almost everyone has a penchant for something sweet, and there's something for everyone with this collection of tasty sweetmeats. Included here are favourites from all over the world – Halva and Stuffed Dates from the Middle East, Kumquats from Italy and Spiced Pears from the United States. Choose from amongst the selection for an interesting gift for someone

special, and keep your own supply of treats to impress your friends: preserved fruits taste fabulous with thick creamy yogurt, or with Baklava – sensually sweet and wickedly morish!

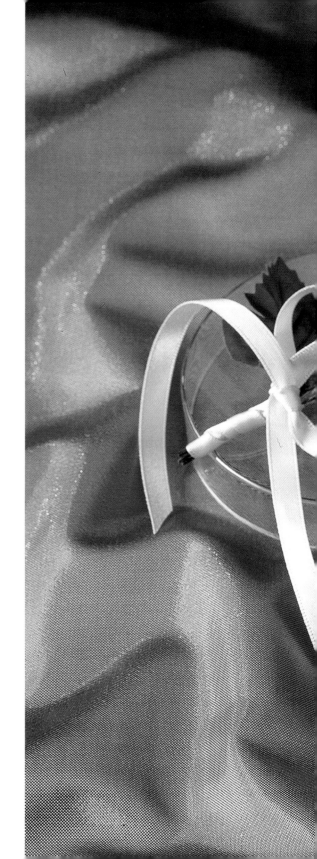

DRIED-FRUIT RUMTOPF

This wonderfully rich and fruity preserve should be stored for at least four weeks to allow the flavours to blend.
For a quick and easy dessert, serve decorated with an orange slice and a sprig of fresh mint.

- 115 g (4 oz/½ cup) granulated sugar
- 225 g (8 oz/2 cups) dried apricots, soaked and drained
- 225 g (8 oz/2 cups) dried apricot halves
- 115 g (4 oz/⅔ cup) dried pitted prunes
- 115 g (4 oz/⅔ cup) semi-dried figs
- 115 g (4 oz/½ cup) dried apple rings
- 225 g (8 oz/1 cup) dried orange rings
- 5 ml (1 tsp) cloves
- 3 sticks cinnamon, halved
- about 350 ml (12 fl oz/1½ cups) dark rum or brandy

1 Put the sugar and 250 ml (8 fl oz/1 cup) water in a pan over a low heat. Stir until the sugar has dissolved and then bring to the boil and boil, without stirring, for 5 minutes. Remove from the heat and set aside to cool.

2 Pack the fruit into three dry, sterilized 450 g (1 lb) jars, arranging the fruit in layers to alternate colours, textures and flavours. Divide the cloves, cinnamon sticks and syrup among the jars and top up with rum or brandy, making sure to cover the fruit.

3 Cover and seal the jars and tip from side to side to blend the liquids. Cool completely and then label and store in a cool place. The fruit should keep well for up to 6 months.

Kumquats and Limequats in Brandy Syrup

These brightly coloured fruits taste very good indeed served with thick creamy yogurt or spooned over vanilla ice-cream.
Make a few extra jars to give to friends and family.

- 450 g (1 lb) kumquats and limequats
- 175 g (6 oz/¾ cup) granulated sugar
- 150 ml (¼ pint/ ⅔ cup) brandy
- 15 ml (1 tbsp) orange-flower water

1 Using a toothpick, prick each individual fruit in several places. Dissolve the sugar in 300 ml (½ pint/ 1¼ cups) water and heat gently, stirring, until the sugar has dissolved.

2 Bring to the boil, then add the fruit and simmer, without stirring, for about 25 minutes until the fruit is tender.

3 Drain the fruit and spoon into hot, dry, sterilized jars. The syrup should be fairly thick: if not, boil for a few minutes, then allow to cool slightly. Stir in the brandy and the orange-flower water, pour over the fruit and seal the jars immediately. Store the preserved fruit in a cool place and use within six months.

Aromatic Spiced Peaches

A great gift for friends who hate cooking, this indulgent dessert is superb served with scoops of luxury vanilla ice cream, drizzled with honey and sprinkled with chopped glacé (preserved) ginger.

- 500 g (1 lb 2 oz/ 2½ cups) granulated sugar
- 12 peaches
- 2 cinnamon sticks
- 4 star anise
- 300 ml (½ pint/ 1¼ cups) brandy

1 Pour 300 ml (½ pint/1¼ cups) water into a saucepan, add the sugar and heat gently, stirring, until dissolved. Bring to the boil and boil for 2 minutes without stirring.

2 Halve and stone the peaches and break the cinnamon sticks in two. Add the peaches, cinnamon sticks and star anise to the syrup, bring back to the boil, then cover and simmer for 5 minutes, turning the peaches once or twice to ensure even cooking.

3 Lift the peaches out with a slotted spoon and pack into two warm, dry, sterilized jars. Divide the spices between the two jars. Boil the remaining sugar syrup rapidly for 5 minutes and pour into the jars to half-fill them. Top up with brandy, making sure that the fruit is completely covered. Add a piece of crumpled greaseproof (wax) paper to keep the fruit beneath the syrup and then seal well. Allow to cool completely, then store in a cool dark place for up to six months before opening.

CINNAMON-SPICED CHERRIES

Make the syrup as above and spice with only 3 cinnamon sticks. Remove the stalks and stones from 1 kg (2¼ lb) cherries, poach in the syrup for 2 minutes and then continue as for the peaches, above.

You may find the fruit will rise to begin with but, as it becomes saturated with the syrup, it will sink back again to the bottom of the jar. Once opened, keep the peaches in the fridge.

Spiced Pears

❦

The Calvados in this sweet and spicy preserve adds a wonderful apple flavour.
The pears are truly excellent served with crêpes, honey and whipped cream.

- 450 g (1 lb/2 cups) granulated sugar
- rind of 1 lemon
- 4 cm (1½ in) piece fresh root ginger
- 1 cinnamon stick
- 10 ml (2 tsp) whole allspice berries
- 1 kg (2¼ lb) hard pears
- cloves
- about 300 ml (½ pint/1¼ cups) Calvados or brandy

1 Pour 600 ml (1 pint/2½ cups) water into a saucepan and add the sugar, lemon rind, ginger, cinnamon stick and allspice berries. Heat over a low heat to dissolve the sugar.

2 Peel the pears, leaving them whole, and stick a clove into each. Add the pears to the pan and simmer for 10–15 minutes until tender.

3 Lift out the pears with a slotted spoon and pack into hot, dry, sterilized jars. Boil the syrup until thickened, pour over the pears and top up with Calvados or brandy, covering the pears completely. Cover tightly and tip the jars gently to mix the liquids. Allow to cool completely, then store the jars in a cool, dark place for up to six months before opening.

ROSE TURKISH DELIGHT

Turkish delight is a traditional Middle Eastern sweet with a delicately perfumed flavour. Serve Turkish style, with tiny cups of strong black coffee.

- 60 ml (4 tbsp) rose water
- 30 ml (2 tbsp) powdered gelatine
- 450 g (1 lb/2 cups) granulated sugar
- red food colouring
- 9 drops rose essential oil

- 25 g (1 oz/¼ cup) roughly chopped blanched almonds
- 20 g (¾ oz/2 tbsp) cornflour (cornstarch)
- 65 g (2½ oz/½ cup) icing (confectioners') sugar

1 Lightly oil a 15–18 cm (6–7 in) baking tin (pan). Pour the rose water into a bowl and sprinkle with the gelatine. Place the sugar in a heavy-based saucepan with 150 ml (¼ pint/⅔ cup) water. Heat gently, stirring, until the sugar has dissolved, then allow to boil, without stirring, until the mixture reaches 119°C (238°F) on a sugar thermometer.

2 Remove the saucepan from the heat and add the gelatine and rose water, stirring until the gelatine has completely dissolved. Add a few drops of red food colouring, then add the rose oil and almonds.

3 Pour the mixture into the prepared baking tin and leave to set.

4 When the mixture is completely set, cut into pieces. Sift the cornflour (cornstarch) and icing (confectioners') sugar together and sprinkle over the cut pieces, then pack in a decorative box.

ALMOND AND HAZELNUT HALVA

Halva is made from semolina and ground hazelnuts, which give it a delicious melt-in-the-mouth quality.

- 115 g (4 oz/ ½ cup) unsalted (sweet) butter, softened
- 115 g (4 oz/½ cup) caster (superfine) sugar
- rind of 1 orange, finely grated
- 30 ml (2 tbsp) fresh orange juice
- 3 eggs
- 175 g (6 oz/1 cup) semolina
- 10 ml (2 tsp) baking powder
- 115 g (4 oz/1 cup) ground hazelnuts

For the topping:
- 350 g (12 oz/ 1½ cups) caster (superfine) sugar
- 2 cinnamon sticks, halved
- juice of 1 lemon
- 60 ml (4 tbsp) orange flower water
- 50 g (2 oz/½ cup) unblanched hazelnuts, toasted and chopped
- 50 g (2 oz/½ cup) blanched almonds, toasted and chopped
- rind of 1 orange, shredded

1 Preheat the oven to 220°C (425°F/Gas 7). Grease the base of a deep 23 cm (9 in) square cake tin (pan) and line it with non-stick baking paper (parchment). Set the tin aside.

3 Turn the mixture into the prepared tin and level the surface with the back of a spoon. Bake in the preheated oven for 20–25 minutes, until just firm and golden. Leave to cool in the tin.

5 Bring to the boil and then boil, without stirring, for 5 minutes. Pour half of the boiling syrup into a separate pan and add the lemon juice and orange flower water. Pour over the halva. Reserve the remaining syrup in the pan.

2 Lightly beat the butter in a bowl until very soft, then add the sugar, orange rind and juice, eggs, semolina, baking powder and hazelnuts and beat together until smooth.

4 To make the syrup, put the sugar in a heavy-based saucepan with 575 ml (18 fl oz/2¼ cups) water and the cinnamon sticks. Heat gently, stirring, until the sugar has dissolved.

6 Leave the halva in the tin until the syrup has been completely absorbed, then turn out on to a plate and cut diagonally into diamond-shaped portions. Scatter with the nuts.

7 Boil the remaining syrup until thickened, then pour over the halva. Scatter the orange rind over the portions. Serve as a dessert with whipped or clotted cream, or pack in boxes for gifts. Halva is best eaten within 2–3 days.

CHOCOLATE APRICOTS

You can use almost any dried fruit for this sophisticated sweetmeat. The sweet but sharp flavour of apricots here contrasts beautifully with the velvet-smooth dark chocolate.

- 50 g (2 oz) plain (semisweet) chocolate
- 12 large dried apricots

To melt this quantity of chocolate in the microwave, put it on a plate and cook on HIGH for about 1 minute. If the chocolate in the bowl starts to set before you have finished dipping all of the apricots, put the bowl back over the heat for a minute or two, or microwave again briefly.

1 Take a length of foil or non-stick baking paper (parchment) and use to line a baking (cookie) sheet. Set the baking sheet aside.

2 Break the chocolate into a double pan or a bowl set over a pan of barely simmering water. Heat until melted, stirring occasionally.

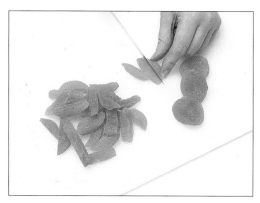

3 Cut each apricot into 2–3 strips. Dip the long cut side of each strip into the melted chocolate and immediately place it on the prepared baking sheet. Chill the chocolates in the freezer for about 30 minutes until set.

4 Use a palette knife to slide the apricots off the foil or baking paper, or press them from underneath. Store the apricots in a cool place, in an airtight container, or pack in a gift box.

GINGERBREAD HEART RING

This table centrepiece is inspired by traditional Polish Christmas decorations. As a variation, you could use other cut-out shapes, such as gingerbread men and women, teddy bears or stars.

For the gingerbread:
- 115 g (4 oz/½ cup) unsalted (sweet) butter, softened
- 50 g (2 oz/¼ cup) caster (superfine) sugar
- 1 egg
- 125 g (4½ oz/ ½ cup) black treacle (molasses)
- 225g (8 oz/2 cups) plain flour
- 5 ml (1 tsp) ground ginger
- 2.5 ml (½ tsp) ground cloves

For the decoration:
- 225 g (8 oz/ 2 cups) icing (confectioners') sugar
- red food colouring
- 30 x 30 cm (12 x 12 in) stiff cardboard
- ribbon
- Victorian-style paper decorations

1 Cream together the butter and sugar until pale and fluffy. Beat in the egg and black treacle (molasses). Sift the flour, ginger and cloves and then beat into the egg and black treacle mixture to make a stiff paste. Turn out on to a lightly floured surface and knead lightly until smooth. Wrap in cellophane (plastic wrap) and chill for 30 minutes. Preheat the oven to 180°C (350°F/Gas 4).

2 Grease two baking (cookie) sheets. Roll out the dough to 1 cm (½ in) thickness and cut out seven heart shapes. Place the hearts on the baking sheets and bake for 10 minutes, until firm. Allow the biscuits to cool on a wire rack. Blend half of the icing (confectioners') sugar with enough warm water to make a fairly thick paste and pipe decorations around the edges of each of the gingerbreads.

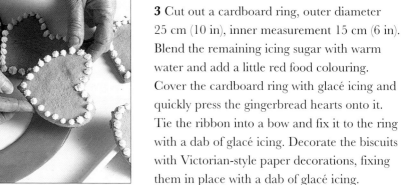

3 Cut out a cardboard ring, outer diameter 25 cm (10 in), inner measurement 15 cm (6 in). Blend the remaining icing sugar with warm water and add a little red food colouring. Cover the cardboard ring with glacé icing and quickly press the gingerbread hearts onto it. Tie the ribbon into a bow and fix it to the ring with a dab of glacé icing. Decorate the biscuits with Victorian-style paper decorations, fixing them in place with a dab of glacé icing.

MARZIPAN FRUITS

*These eye-catching and realistic fruits will make an original gift, which can be used for decorating cakes
or simply enjoyed for themselves as a sweetmeat.*

- 450 g (1 lb) white marzipan
- yellow, green, red, orange and
- burgundy food colouring pastes
- 30 g (2 tbsp) whole cloves

1 Grease a baking (cookie) sheet and line it with non-stick baking paper (parchment). Cut the marzipan into quarters. Reserving three of the quarters, cut the fourth into 10 even-sized pieces and set them aside. Spoon a little of each of the food colouring pastes on to a palette or small plate. Using a sharp kitchen knife, cut two-thirds of the cloves into two pieces, making a stem and a core end from each clove.

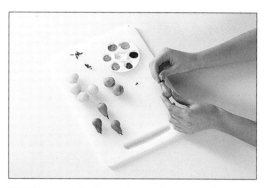

2 Take a small piece of marzipan and shape into a neat ball. Dip a ball in the yellow food colouring and knead between your fingers until evenly coloured. Re-dip into the green colouring and knead lightly to make a green-yellow colour. Using your forefinger, roll one end of the ball to make a pear shape. Press a clove stem into the top and core end into the base. Repeat with the remaining nine balls of marzipan and place on a baking sheet.

3 Cut another piece of marzipan into 10 pieces and shape into balls. Dip each piece into green food colouring and knead to colour evenly. Add a spot of red colouring and roll to blend the colour. Using a ball tool or the end of a paintbrush, indent the top and base to make an apple shape. Insert a stem and core.

4 Repeat as above, using another piece of the marzipan to make 10 orange-coloured balls. Roll each marzipan ball over the surface of a fine grater to give the texture of an orange skin. Press a clove core into the base of each.

5 Take the remaining piece of marzipan, reserve a small piece and colour the rest a deep red using the burgundy food colouring. Mould the red marzipan into lots of tiny marzipan beads. Place a whole clove on the baking sheet and arrange a cluster of burgundy beads into the shape of a bunch of grapes. Repeat with the remaining marzipan beads to make another three bunches of grapes.

6 Roll out the remaining small piece of marzipan and brush with green food colouring. Using a small vine leaf cutter, cut out eight leaves, marking the veins with a knife. Place two leaves on each bunch of grapes, bending them slightly to give a realistic appearance. When all the marzipan fruits are completely dry, pack them in gift boxes.

STUFFED DATES

Slivers of crystallized (candied) ginger give a bite to these fresh dates stuffed with marzipan and topped with halved walnuts. Packed into a decorative box, they make a delightfully exotic gift.

- 24 fresh dates
- 50 g (2 oz) crystallized (candied) ginger
- 115 g (4 oz) marzipan
- 24 walnut halves

1 Using a sharp knife, slit the dates along their length and then carefully remove the stones.

2 Chop the ginger into slivers and work them into the marzipan. Place a walnut-sized piece of marzipan in the cavity of each date and top with a halved walnut.

3 Pack the dates into a decorative box, tied with a length of gold ribbon, if liked. The dates should be stored in the fridge and eaten within one week.

SUGARED FLOWERS

Made in minutes, these pretty decorations add a delightful touch to any light summery dessert, especially fruit soufflés, mousses and trifles. Arrange the flowers on the dessert at the last minute, otherwise they will go soft.

- spring or summer flowers, such as pansies, violas, violets, primroses or roses
- 1–2 egg whites
- caster (superfine) or icing (confectioners') sugar

1 Choose a selection of newly blossomed, unblemished flowers, avoiding any growing near roads, footpaths or where they may have been sprayed with pesticides. Ideally, pick them on a sunny day so that the leaves are dry. If necessary, rinse the petals in cold water and carefully pat them dry with kitchen paper.

2 Lightly beat the egg white, then paint onto the petals with a soft paintbrush. Make sure to reach right into the flower and don't forget to coat the back of the petals. Dust caster (superfine) or icing (confectioners') sugar evenly over the petals, carefully shaking off the excess.

3 Set the flowers on a plate and leave to dry for about 1 hour, then store in shallow boxes, between layers of kitchen paper. Stored in a cool, dry place, sugared flowers will keep for a week. Do not store in the fridge: the damp atmosphere will cause the flowers to wilt.

Fragrant herbs, like variegated mint and sweet cicely, rose or geranium leaves also make pretty decorations.

BAKLAVA

❦

Sweet syrup-soaked pastries are popular in Greece and the Middle East. This version is flavoured with lemon and rose water.

- 200 g (7 oz/1¼ cups) shelled pistachio nuts
- 5 ml (1 tsp) caster (superfine) sugar
- 10 ml (2 tsp) rose water
- 275 g (10 oz) filo pastry
- 45–60 ml (3–4 tbsp) melted butter or sunflower oil

For the syrup:
- 300 g (11 oz/1½ cups) caster (superfine) sugar
- juice of 1 lemon

1 Preheat the oven to 180°C (350°F/Gas 4). Chop the pistachio nuts in a food processor but don't grind them too finely. Stir the sugar and the rose water in with the nuts.

2 Oil a 25 cm (10 in) square baking (cookie) sheet. Cover with a sheet of pastry, brush with butter or oil and then cover with a second sheet. Use up half of the pastry in this way.

3 Spread some of the nut mixture evenly over the pastry and cover with a filo sheet. Repeat until the butter or oil and pastry are used up.

4 Cut vertical lines, 4 cm (1½ in) apart. Cut through the pastry and nuts, then cut diagonal lines to form diamond shapes. Bake for 20 minutes, then reduce the oven temperature to 150°C (300°F/Gas 2) and cook for a further 15–20 minutes. Cool in the tin for 10 minutes.

5 Meanwhile, place 175 ml (6 fl oz/¾ cup) water in a pan, add the sugar and heat gently, stirring, until dissolved. Bring to the boil, add 30 ml (2 tbsp) lemon juice and boil for about 6 minutes, without stirring. Stir in the remaining lemon juice. Leave to cool and thicken slightly.

6 Pour the syrup over the baklava, spreading it evenly with a palette knife. Cover the baklava, still on the sheet, with foil and leave in a cool place for several hours or overnight before turning out, cutting into diamonds and packing into a gift box or airtight container.

INDEX